A WREATH OF
CHRISTMAS POEMS

A WREATH OF CHRISTMAS POEMS

VIRGIL   DANTE   CHAUCER   HERRICK   BEN JONSON

MILTON   WITHER   SOUTHWELL   RILKE   WHITTIER

CHRISTINA ROSSETTI   T. S. ELIOT   LOPE DE VEGA

MARTIN ADAN   PHYLLIS McGINLEY   KENNETH PATCHEN

GRANGER BOOKS
MIAMI, FLORIDA

FIRST PUBLISHED 1942
REPRINTED 1976

PRINTED IN THE UNITED STATES OF AMERICA

THE FOURTH ECLOGUE

VIRGIL

(70 B.C.-19 B.C.)

Surely Virgil's "prophetic" Eclogue must be the oldest of all Christmas poems for it was written about 40 B. C. Actually the poet sang of the coming Golden Age to honor the birth of the son of Pollio, an important Roman politician of the day. But the people of the Middle Ages became convinced that Virgil had had a revelation and was really announcing the birth of the King of Kings. It was the Emperor Constantine himself who first publicized the idea. Later the allegory was developed by the learned scholar Servius and by many others after him. Thus Virgil came to be almost a saint in the minds of Christian writers, and Dante chose him for his guide on the path of salvation in the Divine Comedy. This translation is by J. Laughlin.

Muses
Muses of Sicily
Now let us sing a serious song
There are taller trees than the apple and the crouching tamerisk
If we sing of the woods, let our forest be stately

Now the last age is coming
As it was written in the Sybil's book
The great circle of the centuries begins again
Justice, the Virgin, has returned to earth
With all of Saturn's court
A new line is sent down to us from the skies
And thou, Lucina, must smile
Smile for the birth of the boy, the blessed boy
For whom they will beat their swords into ploughshares
For whom the golden race will rise, the whole world new
Smile, pure Lucina, smile
Thine own Apollo will reign

And thou, Pollio
It is in thy term this glorious age begins
And the great months begin their march
When we shall lose all trace of the old guilt
And the world learn to forget fear
For the boy will become divine
He will see gods and heroes

19316

And will himself be seen by them as god and hero
As he rules over a world of peace
A world made peaceful by his father's wisdom

For thee, little boy, will the earth pour forth gifts
All untilled, give thee gifts
First the wandering ivy and foxglove
Then colocasia and the laughing acanthus
Uncalled the goats will come home with their milk
No longer need the herds fear the lion
Thy cradle itself will bloom with sweet flowers
The serpent will die
The poison plant will wither
Assyrian herbs will spring up everywhere

And when thou art old enough to read of heroes
And of thy father's great deeds
Old enough to understand the meaning of courage
Then will the plain grow yellow with ripe grain
Grapes will grow on brambles
Hard old oaks drip honey

Yet still there must remain some traces of the old guilt
That lust that drives men to taunt the sea with ships
To circle cities with walls
And cut the earth with furrows
There must be another Tiphys
Another Argo carrying picked men
And there must be a war, one final war
With great Achilles storming a last Troy

But when thou hast grown strong and become a man
Then even the trader will leave the sea
His pine ship carry no more wares
And everywhere the land will yield all things that life requires
No longer need the ground endure the harrow
Nor the vine the pruning hook
The farmer can free his oxen from the yoke
Then coloured cloths no longer will need lying dyes
For the ram in the field will change his own fleece

To soft purple or saffron yellow
Each grazing lamb will have a scarlet coat

'Onward, O glorious ages, onward'
Thus sang the fatal sisters to their spindles
Chanting together the unalterable Will

Go forward, little boy, to thy great honours
Soon comes thy time
Dear child of gods from whom a Jupiter will come
See how for thee the world nods its huge head
All lands and seas and endless depths of sky
See how the earth rejoices in the age that is to be

O may my life be long enough to let me sing of thee
With strength enough to tell thy deeds
With such a theme not even Thracian Orpheus could outsing me
Not Linus either, though Apollo prompted him
Help from Calliope herself could not make Orpheus' song the best
And even Pan, with Arcady as judge
Yes Pan, would fall before me when I sang of thee

Learn, little boy, to greet thy mother with a smile
For thee she has endured nine heavy months
Learn, little boy, to smile
For if thou didst not smile
And if thy parents did not smile on thee
No god could ask thee to his table
No goddess to her bed.

ST. BERNARD'S HYMN TO THE VIRGIN

DANTE
(1265-1321)

Of the countless poems written in praise of the Virgin by far the most wonderful is that which Dante puts in the mouth of St. Bernard in the final canto of the Divine Comedy. No translation could possibly do justice to its perfection, so we give the original Italian, followed by a rough prose paraphrase.

Vergine Madre, figlia del tuo Figlio,
  Umile e alta più che creatura,
  Termine fisso d'etterno consiglio,

Tu se' colei che l'umana natura
  Nobilitasti sì che il suo Fattore
  Non disdegnò di farsi sua fattura.

Nel ventre tuo si raccese l'amore
  Per lo cui caldo ne l'etterna pace
  Così è germinato questo fiore.

Qui sei a noi meridiana face
  Di caritate, e giuso intra i mortali
  Se' di speranza fontana vivace.

Donna, se' tanto grande e tanto vali
  Che qual vuol grazia ed a te non ricorre,
  Sua disianza vuol volar sanz' ali.

La tua benignità non pur soccorre
  A chi domanda, ma molte fiate
  Liberamente al dimandar precorre.

In te misericordia, in te pietate,
  In te magnificenza, in te s'aduna
  Quantunque in creatura è di bontate.

Virgin Mother, daughter of thine own Son, so humble yet more exalted than any creature, fixed goal of the eternal plan, thou art she who did so raise our human nature that its own Creator was not ashamed to take its form. In thee was born the love whose warmth has grown this flower in the timeless peace. In heaven thou art the noonday torch of charity and below on mortal earth thou art the living fountain of hope. Lady, thou art so great and such is thy power that he who seeks grace and does not turn for it to thee leaves his desire trying to fly without wings. Such is thy kindness that it helps not only those who ask but often freely goes before and helps before the asking. In thee mercy, pity, magnificence and whatever goodness exists in any creature are joined together.

CHAUCER

(1340-1400)

Chaucer was thoroughly familiar with the works of Dante and often paraphrased him in his own poetry. Here are the sixth, seventh and eighth stanzas of Chaucer's Second Nun's Tale, *which are based almost entirely on Dante's hymn.*

Thou mayde and mooder, doghter of thy sone,
Thou welle of mercy, sinful soules cure,
In whom that god for bountee, chees to wone,
Thou humble, and heigh over every creature,
Thou nobledest so forforth our nature,
That no desdeyn the maker hadde of kinde,
His sone in blode and flesh to clothe and winde.

Withinne the cloistre blisful of thy sydes
Took mannes shap the eternal love and pees,
That of the tryne compas lord and gyde is,
Whom erthe and see and heven, out of relees,
Ay herien: and thou, virgin wemmelees,
Bar of thy body, and dweltest mayden pure,
The creatour of every creature.

Assembled is in thee magnificence
With mercy, goodnesse, and with swich pitee
That thou, that art the sonne of excellence,
Nat only helpest hem that preyen thee,
But ofte tyme, of thy benignitee,
Ful frely, er that men thyn help biseche,
Thou goost biforn, and art hir lyves leche.

("wone"—dwell. "ferforth"—far. "tryne compas"—threefold world. "out of relees"—without ceasing. "Ay berien"—ever praise. "wemmelees"—stainless. "leche"—physician.)

AS DEW IN APRIL

(ANONYMOUS—FIFTEENTH CENTURY)

I sing of a maiden
That is makeless;
King of all kings
To her son she ches.

He came all so still
There his mother was,
As dew in April
That falleth on the grass.

He came all so still
To his mother's bower,
As dew in April
That falleth on the flower.

He came all so still
There his mother lay,
As dew in April
That falleth on the spray.

Mother and maiden
Was never none but she;
Well may such a lady
Goddes mother be.

("makeless"—matchless. "ches"—chose.)

THE BURNING BABE

ROBERT SOUTHWELL
(1561-1595)

As I in hoary winter's night stood shivering in the snow,
Surprised I was with sudden heat which made my heart to glow;

And lifting up a fearful eye to view what fire was near,
A pretty Babe all burning bright did in the air appear,

Who scorched with excessive heat such floods of tears did shed,
As though his floods should quench his flames which with his tears
    were fed.

"Alas!" quoth he, "but newly born in fiery heats, I fry,
Yet none approach to warm their hearts or feel my fire but I!

My faultless heart the furnace is, the fuel wounding thorns;
Love is the fire and sighs the smoke, the ashes shame and scorns;

The fuel Justice layeth on, and Mercy blows the coals;
The metal in this furnace wrought are men's defiled souls;

For which, as now on fire I am, to work them to their good,
So will I melt into a bath to wash them in my blood."

With that he vanished out of sight and swiftly shrunk away,
And straightway I called into mind that it was Christmas Day.

NEW PRINCE, NEW POMP

ROBERT SOUTHWELL
(1561-1595)

Behold, a seely tender babe
   In freezing winter night
In homely manger trembling lies—
   Alas, a piteous sight!

The inns are full, no man will yield
   This little pilgrim bed,
But forced he is with seely beasts
   In crib to shroud his head.

Despise him not for lying there;
   First, what he is enquire.
An orient pearl is often found
   In depth of dirty mire.

Weigh not his crib, his wooden dish,
   Nor beasts that by him feed;
Weigh not his mother's poor attire
   Nor Joseph's simple weed.

This stable is a prince's court,
   This crib his chair of state,
The beasts are parcel of his pomp,
   The wooden dish his plate.

The persons in that poor attire
   His royal liveries wear;
The prince himself is come from heaven—
   This pomp is prizëd there.

With joy approach, O Christian wight;
   Do homage to thy king;
And highly prize his humble pomp
   Which he from heaven doth bring.

A SONG OF THE VIRGIN MOTHER

LOPE DE VEGA
(1562-1635)

As ye go through these palm-trees
O holy angels;
Sith sleepeth my child here
Still ye the branches.

O Bethlehem palm-trees
That move to the anger
Of winds in their fury,
Tempestuous voices,
Make ye no clamor,
Run ye less swiftly,
Sith sleepeth the child here
Still ye your branches.

He the divine child
Is here a-wearied
Of weeping the earth-pain,
Here for his rest would he
Cease from his mourning,
Only a little while,
Sith sleepeth this child here
Stay ye the branches.

Cold be the fierce winds,
Treacherous round him.
Ye see that I have not
Wherewith to guard him,
O angels, divine ones
That pass us a-flying,
Sith sleepeth my child here
Stay ye the branches.

Translated from the Spanish by Ezra Pound

A HYMN ON THE NATIVITY
OF MY SAVIOUR

BEN JONSON
(1573-1637)

I sing the birth was born tonight,
The author both of life and light;
 The angels so did sound it.
And like the ravished shepherds said,
Who saw the light and were afraid,
 Yet searched, and true they found it.

The Son of God, the eternal king,
That did us all salvation bring,
 And freed the soul from danger:
He whom the whole world could not take,
The Word, which heaven and earth did make,
 Was now laid in a manger.

The Father's wisdom willed it so,
The Son's obedience knew no No,
 Both wills were in one stature;
And as that wisdom had decreed,
The Word was now made flesh indeed,
 And took on Him our nature.

What comfort by Him do we win,
Who made Himself the price of sin,
 To make us heirs of glory!
To see this babe all innocence,
A martyr born in our defence—
 Can man forget the story?

A CHRISTMAS CAROL

GEORGE WITHER
(1588-1667)

So now is come our joyfullest feast,
Let every man be jolly;
Each room with ivy leaves is dressed,
And every post with holly.
  Though some churls at our mirth repine,
  Round your foreheads garlands twine,
  Drown sorrow in a cup of wine,
And let us all be merry.

Now all our neighbors' chimneys smoke,
And Christmas blocks are burning;
Their ovens they with baked meats choke,
And all their spits are turning.
  Without the door let sorrow lie;
  And if for cold it hap to die,
  We'll bury it in a Christmas pie,
And evermore be merry.

Now every lad is wondrous trim,
And no man minds his labor;
Our lasses have provided them
A bagpipe and a tabor.
  Young men and maids, and girls and boys,
  Give life to one another's joys;
  And you anon shall by their noise
Perceive that they are merry.

Rank misers now do sparing shun:
Their hall of music soundeth,
And dogs thence with whole shoulders run—
So all things there aboundeth.
  The country folk themselves advance,
  For Crowdy-mutton's come out of France,
  And Jack shall pipe, and Jill shall dance,
And all the town be merry.

Ned Swash hath fetched his bands from pawn,
And all his best apparel;
Brisk Nell hath bought a ruff of lawn,
With dropping of the barrel.
  And those that hardly all the year
  Had bread to eat, or rags to wear,
  Will have both clothes and dainty fare,
And all the day be merry.

Now poor men to the justices
With capons make their arrants;
And if they hap to fail of these,
They plague them with their warrants.
  But now they feed them with good cheer,
  And what they want they take in beer:
  For Christmas comes but once a year,
And then they shall be merry.

Good farmers in the country nurse
The poor, that else were undone;
Some landlords spend their money worse
On lust and pride at London.
  There the roisters they do play,
  Drab and dice their lands away;
  Which may be ours another day,
And therefore let's be merry.

The client now his suit forbears,
The prisoner's heart is eased,
The debtor drinks away his cares
And, for the time, is pleased.
  Though others' purses be more fat,
  Why should we pine or grieve at that?
  Hang sorrow, care will kill a cat;
And therefore let's be merry.

Hark how the wags abroad do call
Each other forth to rambling;
Anon, you'll see them in the Hall
For nuts and apples scambling.
  Hark how the roofs with laughter sound!
  Anon they'll think the house goes round,
  For they the cellar's depth have found,
And there they will be merry.

The wenches with their wassail bowls
About the streets are singing;
The boys are come to catch the owls
The Wild-mare in is bringing.
  Our kitchen boy hath broke his box,
  And to the dealing of the ox
  Our honest neighbors come by flocks,
And here they will be merry.

Now kings and queens poor sheep-cotes have
And mate with everybody;
The honest now may play the knave,
And wise men play at noddy.
  Some youths will now a-mumming go;
  Some others play at Rowland-Ho,
  And twenty other gamboys mo,
Because they will be merry.

Then wherefore in these merry days
Should we, I pray, be duller?
No; let us sing some roundelays
To make our mirth the fuller.
  And whilest thus inspired we sing,
  Let all the streets with echoes ring;
  Woods and hills and everything
Bear witness we are merry.

TO HIS SAVIOUR, A CHILD;
A PRESENT, BY A CHILD

ROBERT HERRICK
(1591-1674)

Go, pretty child, and bear this flower
Unto thy little Saviour;
And tell Him, by that bud now blown,
He is the Rose of Sharon known.
When thou hast said so, stick it there
Upon his bib or stomacher;
And tell Him, for good handsel too,
That thou hast brought a whistle new,
Made of a clean straight oaten reed,
To charm his cries at time of need.
Tell Him, for coral, thou hast none,
But if thou hadst, He should have one;
But poor thou art, and known to be
Even as moneyless as He.
Lastly, if thou canst win a kiss
From those mellifluous lips of His,
Then never take a second on
To spoil the first impression.

CEREMONIES FOR CHRISTMAS

ROBERT HERRICK

Come, bring with a noise,
My merry merry boys,
The Christmas Log to the firing;
While my good dame, she
Bids ye all be free,
And drink to your hearts' desiring.

With the last year's brand
Light the new block, and,
For good success in his spending,
On your psalt'ries play,
That sweet luck may
Come while the Log is a-teending.

Drink now the strong beer,
Cut the white loaf here,
The while the meat is a-shredding;
For the rare mince-pie
And the plums stand by
To fill the paste that's a-kneading

ON THE MORNING OF CHRIST'S NATIVITY

(abridged)

JOHN MILTON

(1608-1674)

I

This is the month, and this the happy morn,
Wherein the Son of Heaven's eternal King,
Of wedded maid and virgin mother born,
Our great redemption from above did bring;
For so the holy sages once did sing,
    That He our deadly forfeit should release,
And with His Father work us a perpetual peace.

II

That glorious Form, that Light unsufferable,
And that far-beaming blaze of Majesty,
Wherewith He wont at Heaven's high council-table
To sit the midst of Trinal Unity,
He laid aside; and here with us to be
    Forsook the courts of everlasting day,
And chose with us a darksome house of mortal clay.

Say Heavenly Muse, shall not thy sacred vein.
Afford a present to the Infant God?
Hast thou no verse, no hymn, or solemn strain,
To welcome Him to this His new abode,
Now while the Heaven, by the Sun's team untrod,
    Hath took no print of the approaching light,
And all the spangled host keep watch in squadrons bright?

IV

See how from far upon the eastern road
The star-led wizards haste with odours sweet!
O run, prevent them with thy humble ode,
And lay it lowly at His blessed feet;
Have thou the honour first thy Lord to greet,
    And join thy voice unto the angel quire,
From out His secret altar touched with hallowed fire.

THE HYMN

I

It was the winter wild,
While the Heaven-born Child
    All meanly wrapt in the rude manger lies;
Nature in awe to Him
Had doffed her gaudy trim,
    With her great Master so to sympathize:
It was no season then for her
To wanton with the sun her lusty paramour.

II

Only with speeches fair
She woos the gentle air
    To hide her guilty front with innocent snow,
And on her naked shame,
Pollute with sinful blame,
    The saintly veil of maiden white to throw,
Confounded, that her Maker's eyes
Should look so near upon her foul deformities.

III

But He, her fears to cease,
Sent down the meek-eyed Peace;
　　She crowned with olive green came softly sliding
Down through the turning sphere,
His ready harbinger,
　　With turtle wing the amorous clouds dividing,
And waving wide her myrtle wand,
She strikes a universal peace through sea and land.

IV

No war or battle's sound
Was heard the world around,
　　The idle spear and shield were high up-hung:
The hooked chariot stood
Unstained with hostile blood,
　　The trumpet spake not to the armed throng,
And kings sat still with awful eye,
As if they surely knew their sovran Lord was by.

V

But peaceful was the night
Wherein the Prince of Light
　　His reign of peace upon the earth began:
The winds with wonder whist,
Smoothly the waters kissed,
　　Whispering new joys to the mild Ocean,
Who now hath quite forgot to rave,
While birds of calm sit brooding on the charmed wave.

VI

The stars with deep amaze
Stand fixed in steadfast gaze,
　　Bending one way their precious influence,
And will not take their flight,
For all the morning light,
　　Or Lucifer that often warned them thence;
But in their glimmering orbs did glow,
Until their Lord Himself bespake, and bid them go.

VII

And though the shady gloom
Had given day her room,
   The sun himself withheld his wonted speed,
And hid his head for shame,
As his inferior flame
   The new-enlightened world no more should need;
He saw a greater Sun appear
Than his bright throne or burning axle-tree could bear

VIII

The shepherds on the lawn,
Or ere the point of dawn,
   Sat simply chatting in a rustic row;
Full little thought they then
That the mighty Pan
   Was kindly come to live with them below;
Perhaps their loves or else their sheep,
Was all that did their silly thoughts so busy keep.

IX

When such music sweet
Their hearts and ears did greet,
   As never was by mortal finger strook,
Divinely warbled voice
Answering the stringed noise,
   As all their souls in blissful rapture took:
The air such pleasure loth to lose,
With thousand echoes still prolongs each heavenly close.

X

Nature that heard such sound
Beneath the hollow round
   Of Cynthia's seat, the airy region thrilling,
Now was almost won
To think her part was done,
   And that her reign had here its last fulfilling;
She knew such harmony alone
Could hold all Heaven and Earth in happier union.

THE MYSTIC'S CHRISTMAS

JOHN GREENLEAF WHITTIER
(1807-1892)

"All hail!" the bells of Christmas rang,
"All hail!" the monks at Christmas sang,
The merry monks who kept with cheer
The gladdest day of all their year.

But still apart, unmoved thereat,
A pious elder brother sat
Silent, in his accustomed place,
With God's sweet peace upon his face.

"Why sitt'st thou thus?" his brethren cried.
"It is the blessed Christmas-tide;
The Christmas lights are all aglow,
The sacred lilies bud and blow.

"Above our heads the joy-bells ring,
Without the happy children sing,
And all God's creatures hail the morn
On which the holy Christ was born!

"Rejoice with us; no more rebuke
Our gladness with thy quiet look."
The gray monk answered: "Keep, I pray,
Even as ye list, the Lord's birthday.

"Let heathen Yule fires flicker red
Where thronged refectory feasts are spread;
With mystery-play and masque and mime
And wait-songs speed the holy time!

"The blindest faith may haply save;
The Lord accepts the things we have;
And reverence, howsoe'er it strays,
May find at last the shining ways.

"They needs must grope who cannot see,
The blade before the ear must be;
As ye are feeling I have felt,
And where ye dwell I too have dwelt.

"But now, beyond the things of sense,
Beyond occasions and events,
I know, through God's exceeding grace,
Release from form and time and place.

"I listen, from no mortal tongue,
To hear the song the angels sung;
And wait within myself to know
The Christmas lilies bud and blow.

"The outward symbols disappear
From him whose inward sight is clear;
And small must be the choice of days
To him who fills them all with praise!

"Keep while you need it, brothers mine,
With honest zeal your Christmas sign,
But judge not him who every morn
Feels in his heart the Lord Christ born!"

A CHRISTMAS CAROL

CHRISTINA ROSSETTI

(1830-1894)

Before the paling of the stars,
   Before the winter morn,
Before the earliest cock-crow
   Jesus Christ was born:
   Born in a stable,
   Cradled in a manger,
In the world His hands had made
   Born a stranger.

Priest and king lay fast asleep
   In Jerusalem,
Young and old lay fast asleep
   In crowded Bethlehem:
Saint and angel, ox and ass,
   Kept a watch together,
Before the Christmas daybreak
   In the winter weather.

Jesus on His mother's breast
   In the stable cold,
Spotless Lamb of God was He,
   Shepherd of the fold:
Let us kneel with Mary maid,
   With Joseph bent and hoary,
With saint and angel, ox and ass,
   To hail the King of Glory.

JOSEPH'S SUSPICION

RAINER MARIA RILKE
(1875-1926)

And the angel, taking some pains, told
Considerately the man who clenched his fists:
"But can't you see in her robe's every fold
That she is cool as the Lord's morning mists?"

But the other murmured, looking sinister:
"What is it that has wrought this change in her?"
Then cried the angel to him: "Carpenter,
Can't you see yet that God is acting here?"

"Because you plane the planks, of your pride could
You really make the Lord God answerable,
Who unpretentiously from the same wood
Makes the leaves burst forth, the young buds swell?"

He understood that. And then as he raised
His frightened glance toward the angel who
Had gone away . . . slowly the man drew
Off his heavy cap. Then in song he praised.

Translated by C. F. MacIntyre

NATIVITY

MARTIN ADAN
(PERU)

Your eyes
join hands
like the Madonnas
of Leonardo.

The groves of sunset,
purple foliage
of a shadowy Renaissance.

The flock of the sea
bleats at the cavern
of a sky full of angels.

God is made flesh
in a child that gropes for the toys
of your hands.

Your lips
give the warmth denied
by donkey and cow.

And in the half light
your hair spreads its straw
for the Infant God.

Translated by Muna Lee

JOURNEY OF THE MAGI

T. S. ELIOT

'A cold coming we had of it,
Just the worst time of the year
For a journey, and such a long journey:
The ways deep and the weather sharp,
The very dead of winter.'
And the camels galled, sore-footed, refractory,
Lying down in the melting snow.
There were times we regretted
The summer palaces on slopes, the terraces,
And the silken girls bringing sherbet.
Then the camel men cursing and grumbling
And running away, and wanting their liquor and women,
And the night-fires going out, and the lack of shelters,
And the cities hostile and the towns unfriendly
And the villages dirty and charging high prices:
A hard time we had of it.
At the end we preferred to travel all night,
Sleeping in snatches,
With the voices singing in our ears, saying
That this was all folly.

Then at dawn we came down to a temperate valley,
Wet, below the snow line, smelling of vegetation;
With a running stream and a water-mill beating the darkness,
And three trees on the low sky,
And an old white horse galloped away in the meadow.
Then we came to a tavern with vine-leaves over the lintel,
Six hands at an open door dicing for pieces of silver,
And feet kicking the empty wine-skins.
But there was no information, and so we continued
And arrived at evening, not a moment too soon
Finding the place; it was (you may say) satisfactory.

All this was a long time ago, I remember,
And I would do it again, but set down
This set down

This: were we led all that way for
Birth or Death? There was a Birth, certainly,
We had evidence and no doubt. I had seen birth and death,
But had thought they were different; this birth was
Hard and bitter agony for us, like Death, our death.
We returned to our places, these Kingdoms,
But no longer at ease here, in the old dispensation,
With an alien people clutching their gods.
I should be glad of another death.

I HAVE LIGHTED THE CANDLES, MARY

KENNETH PATCHEN

I have lighted the candles, Mary . . .
How softly breathes your little Son

My wife has spread the table
With our best cloth. There are apples,
Bright as red clocks, upon the mantel.
The snow is a weary face at the window.
How sweetly does He sleep

"Into this bitter world, O Terrible Huntsman!"
I say, and she takes my hand—"Hush,
You will wake Him."

The taste of tears is on her mouth
When I kiss her. I take an apple
And hold it tightly in my fist;
The cold, swollen face of war leans in the window.

They are blowing out the candles, Mary . . .
The world is a thing gone mad tonight.
O hold Him tenderly, dear Mother,
For His is a kingdom in the hearts of men.

THE HOLY CITY

PHYLLIS McGINLEY

Jerusalem—Bugles which formerly heralded the Sabbath have been replaced by bells and town criers so that there will be no possibility of confusion with air-raid sirens. Palestine's first rationing measure went into effect yesterday.—The Times

In Palestine, in Palestine,
   The flocks unsheltered sleep,
Though night-long still
On every hill
   A watch the shepherds keep.

And people walk with living fear
   Lest, singing while it fell,
Should shine upon some midnight clear
   The star that is a shell.

The bells ring out in Palestine,
   Where there's a sentry stationed,
And still the oil and still the wine
   Are blessed before they're rationed,

And criers chant the Sabbath for
   The faithful and the stranger,
But now the bugles blow no more
   Except the song of danger.

Lower your gates, Jerusalem.
   Make mute the sacred horn,
While dark comes down
Upon that town
   Wherein the Light was born.

"A Wreath Of Christmas Poems," edited by Albert M. Hayes and James Laughlin, was designed and printed by Maurice Serle Kaplan at the Blue Ox Press. The types used are Weiss and Lydian.

THE POETS OF THE YEAR

These booklets of poetry are issued twelve times yearly and may be had singly or by annual subscription. The Series for the year 1942 is listed on the back cover flap. That for 1941 and that planned for 1943 are listed here below. Each number is individually designed and printed at a different fine press.

1941

"The Broken Span" by William Carlos Williams
"The End Of A Decade" by Harry Brown
"Some Poems & A Devotion" of John Donne
"The Paradox In The Circle" by Theodore Spencer
"Poems On Several Occasions" by Josephine Miles
"Shenandoah" a verse play by Delmore Schwartz
"The Giant Weapon" by John Wheelwright
"A Letter From The Country" by Howard Baker
"Poems From The Book Of Hours" by Rainer Maria Rilke
"More Poems From The Palatine Anthology" by Dudley Fitts
"The Dry Season" by Malcolm Cowley
"Poems" by F. T. Prince

1943

"An Anthology of War Poetry" edited by Richard Eberhart
"Some Poems of Hoelderlin" translated by Frederic Prokosch
"A Satire Against Mankind & Other Poems" by the Earl of Rochester
"Selected Poems" by Yvor Winters
"The Illuminations of Rimbaud" translated by E. Rootham
"Ballads of Buenos Aires" collected by Lincoln Kirstein
"New Poems" by Dylan Thomas
"Three Russian Poets" (Pushkin, Lermontov, Tutchev) translated by V. Nabokov
"And You, Thoreau" by August Derleth
"The Death of Lucullus" a verse play by Bertolt Brecht
"Selected Poems" of Herman Melville
"Poems" by Richard Eberhart